How to

START A BUSINESS

With NO MONEY

By

Delyen Madula

Acknowledgment

Special thanks to Tom, to my family, and to my spiritual family who helped me through during the lowest point of my life. To Tito Henry Fernandez, who's been like a Father to us.

Table of Contents

Introduction

This book will reinforce your belief that it is, without question, possible for ordinary people like me and you, to make good entrepreneurs, and be financially free.

This book is for those who aspires to change. From ordinary to extraordinary. From weakness to strength. From desolation to freedom from it.

"You will not know how strong you are until being strong is the only choice you have"

This book does not promise an immediate change, nor a quick-rich formula. But it will surely give you insights from real life examples that will aid you to start your own business even with no money.

Chapter 1

Take care of the basics

Have you often envied the lifestyle and status of your friends posting happy moments, travels, and successes in social media?

Do you wish you could also drive the luxury car they are driving; own the same expensive house they own or better; own the same gadgets they are flaunting or something better; and if you are a woman, are you dying to get the same beautiful dresses, bags and accessories, your friends so proudly wear?

Did you already get to the point where you no longer check your social media accounts because it became so depressing?

Have you justified this sentiment by telling your friends that you don't like checking your social media account because you find all posts nonsense?

There is only one problem with that: most of your friends or family members, officemates, and clients, made Facebook indispensable. Social media has now become a medium of communication, and most of the time, a business platform.

Is your career not taking off well, and you found yourself comparing your achievements with that of your friends who are now Managers and C-level executives in their respective jobs, or are now successful entrepreneurs in a flourishing industry or profession, while you on the other hand, are still a struggling officer or managerial level, or rank and file employee?

If you are this person, why do you think that is the case for you? Is it because:

You sucked at your job?

Or because you are the typical querulous employee who articulates his complaining a lot, your bosses detest you, but couldn't fire you without violating labor laws?

Or you just don't go the extra mile to get noticed and no good backers to help you up?

Maybe you are not progressing as an employee because you are in the wrong place, occupying the wrong position. You don't serve your purpose. You are like a fish who is forced to fly. You must be thrown into the ocean to unleash your full potential.

In the following chapters, you will be able to determine whether you are cut out to be an entrepreneur or not.

What are your basics?

The minimum requirements of a household for a decent standard of life are: adequate food, shelter, and clothing plus some household equipment and furniture.

Are those things you desired earlier really important?

Basic needs are your essentials, your "non-negotiables", such as food, shelter, and clothing.

Under those major basic needs are their necessary components. Such as, electricity and water under shelter; refrigerator and cooking equipment under food, among others. People who neglect these things can go on with a repetitive episodes of cut-out electricity supply or cut-out water supply once every 3 to 6 months.

Those things that do not fall under the basic needs: food, shelter and clothing are your wants. Your non-essentials. Things that you can live without.

However, there are some who consider internet connection as part of their basic needs, under shelter. It is, for them, something that they can't live without. Most especially if they are in a long distance relationship with their spouses who work abroad. They need the internet connection to constantly communicate with their love ones.

It is up to you to identify and label your needs and wants. An air conditioning unit, for example, is not a basic need, you can live without it, you can sleep without it. But for parents who have infants, ACU is a basic need. Also for a night shift employee who sleeps at daytime and works at nighttime, ACU is important for a comfortable sleep.

Now, if you have identified your needs, can you put the amount corresponding to each item? Sum it all up. Is your current income enough to cover the amount?

If your answer is no, you need to make the necessary adjustments.

Prioritize Your Basics

Make sure to have all your basic needs covered. That is your foundation. Your foundation must be strong enough. If it is weak or broken, everything else will crumble.

You need a comfortable house to sleep in, not necessarily a luxurious one, but comfortable enough to provide you a place to think freely and clearly. Free from oppression and stress.

If you are living in a mortgaged or rented house and you defaulted payment, because you did not prioritize it, and collection agents started harassing you, threatening you with foreclosure, to force you to pay, will you be at peace living in that house?

No. Instead of you focusing on more productive things, you will be pre-occupied with the thought that anytime soon, you will no longer have a house to go home to.

Your house is your refuge, the ultimate place where you don't need any adjusting to do for the benefit of others. In your house, you are "The King" or "The Queen". You are your own boss. Protect your territory.

If you can't afford an entire house yet, get a room just for yourself where you can be alone peacefully.

For you to think clearly, it is very important that your home is free from stress or oppression. Though sometimes we cannot avoid it, and would seem impossible, most especially for married couples with children.

A married friend I know, arranged with her husband that her refuge (the wife) must be in the kitchen, while the husband's refuge is in the garage. If she or her husband wants to be alone, the entire household must respect their privacy.

Some mothers I know take the Comfort Room as their place of refuge.

In case you are a single person, living with your family or relatives, and you really have to adjust as you need to consider their convenience as well, find a place of refuge elsewhere. A place where you can be yourself, where you can think clearly and comfortably.

It could be at work, in the car, jeepney, fx, MRT, or bus while travelling. If it is really hard, make it your goal to acquire a place for yourself very soon.

If you are working now, and you think your income can already support your need for a personal space, get on with it as soon as possible. You will never learn to manage your own life if you still depend on other people for your basic needs.

If you already have your own house, congratulations, you are way ahead.

However, if your income cannot support your basics, you can either:

Increase your income

or

Adjust and decrease your basics.

Most of us do not want to compromise our comfort just because we cannot afford it. So we work on our means, we do our best to increase our income, instead of adjusting our basics.

When I was still an employee, I had a boss who always tells me to look for a cheaper place to live. To consider bed-spacing to cut the cost. That was because, years ago, when I was still in sales, I couldn't meet my sales target. I hardly reach my quota.

I was so broke, struggling with all my bills, monthly living expenses, and law school expenses.

Despite all that, I told my boss that I cannot compromise my basics. I really need a personal space for my studies and for myself.

When I graduated from college, I vowed to myself that when I get a job, I will get a room for myself. I always have trouble with roommates. I no longer want to adjust. I want a space for myself. Attaining that, for me, was already an achievement.

"I will not let my basics adjust to my income. My income should adjust to my basics."

Of course, it was not easy. That requires money, and it did not happen overnight. It took time.

While others seemed to have everything in an instance, we really don't know what struggles they went through behind the scene. We can only see the outcome, not the process.

They might have started early. Discovered the right way to achieve their dreams early.

But keep in mind that we are not the same. Every single person is different. We build our own lives. We write our own stories. We will have our time, in our own pace.

But you have the power to make significant changes in your life. People around you may ridicule you or support you. Nevertheless, continue to strive for what you want and let your success speak for you.

There's no such thing as luck, only opportunity meeting preparedness.

Chapter 2

What are you good at?

I started my first business WITH NOTHING. I didn't know what I was good at. Remember the boss who told me to look for a cheaper place? That same boss was also the reason why I resigned from my previous company.

I couldn't understand her. Maybe because I also have an attitude problem. I don't follow rules if I find it ridiculous, or if I don't agree with its principles. But she was a good sales person. She can sell millions. I really admire her for that. She was good and very helpful too.

After I resigned, I transferred to another company, still in sales. But the product was so hard to sell. Then I realized that I was not really good at selling something that I don't believe in.

I became so frustrated, I cannot seem to make things work in my life. I cannot even sustain my needs. How much more getting what I want?

So I was so determined to get out of my misery. My need to increase my income became so intense that I transformed into a voracious reader. I read every financial book, business book, and mental toughness book I can find.

If one author recommends another author or book, I will find that book. If that recommended author recommends another author, I will look for it also.

I can't stop myself from learning. I thought it was the only hope I had. I educated myself. I always tell myself that there is nothing special about Henry Sy, Gokongwie, and other rich people. They're just humans, if they can do it, why can't I.

Though I don't really aim to be like them. My intention has been just to have more than enough to live a comfortable life and be able to help others.

I need to increase my income. I don't want to struggle for the rest of my life. I am so tired of not having enough, of not getting what I want. Of not being able to extend a hand whenever someone asks for my help.

And then I came across the book of Robert Kiyosaki, "rich dad poor dad". This book triggered lots of ideas in my mind. I began to question myself. What is it really that I am good at?

To be honest, I didn't really know. I cannot give myself an answer that time. I didn't seem to have anything that I was good at.

But I told myself, maybe "I was cut out to be an entrepreneur". If I am my own boss, I can do anything I want. I can make my own marketing campaign (something I think I was good at), sales strategy and sell any products I want. No one will restrict me. It would be fun. And I will be my own boss. I will not report to anyone. The last sentence was the most motivational self-talk I had.

So I read a lot, researched a lot.

I was resolved to become an entrepreneur.

As I go on with my readings, I learned that **you don't actually need money to start a business.** You just need a product or a service that is saleable, and be a good salesman yourself.

Voila! I can be a good salesman.

So I looked for a product or services to sell.

Tom's family, my then friend and now my partner, was in a demolition business. But because of mismanagement, they got bankrupt. I asked him if we (he and I) can continue their family's business. With his Mom's permission, we went on with the business.

So we started pushing and selling the demolition services. We have everything we needed. Their workers who were just waiting for job orders, were still intact, and just a call away. All we needed to do was to sell the services. So I did my best to sell the services, with Tom as my back up support, telling me everything that I needed to know.

It took me some time to grasp everything as it was a new animal for me.

In the course of our business transaction, clients started to entrust to us their rubbish or scrap disposal as well, which we likewise subcontracted with a third party hauler. Hauling transactions kept on coming in, we could really say that everything went well. I did all the sales job, while Tom functioned as my driver.

Out of those activities and transactions, I discovered that I was doing great at negotiations. We got ourselves a deal which I never thought I could close until I was left with no choice but to push harder.

Since the demolition services was not so in demand at that time, as most of our clients were developing empty grounds, hauling services became the new trend. Tom will have to manage the loading and collection, which most of the time took place from 10:00 pm to 4:00 in the morning. The only allowable time to collect debris in Metro Manila.

We were really in such a favorable situation during that time that we did not spend any amount of money in our operation. We contracted the hauler for a weekly payment, while we get the contract from the client in a pay per truck immediate payment. We even have a week to use the money for other transactions.

We did well. But I didn't stop there. I look for another business.

We generated enough money from our hauling services, but the transactions became so stressful and it also deteriorated Tom's health as he needed to oversee everything every single night.

Meanwhile, during one of our casual discussions, Tom mentioned that he wanted to open a T-shirt printing business and that he will pattern it after his bar. He, by the way, operated his own reggae bar, before the Government took over the place and closed it down.

"If you want to engage in business, engage in something that you are really good at."

At that time, Tom, who is a computer engineer by profession, owned cell phone shops that also provide computer services, cabling and CCTV system installations on the side. He has been doing it for eight years, on referral basis and walk-ins only.

So it dawned on me that instead of a T-shirt printing business, why don't he partner with me and grow his current business into an IT company instead.

"You only need three kinds of individuals to start a business, a lawyer, an accountant, and a person who knows your products and services."

I can handle the legal and the accounting aspect of the business, while Tom can take care of the Technical aspects.

It was a perfect set up.

We were already in a spiritual renewal that time, so we see to it that all our actions were properly discerned and blessed by the Lord.

And so out of the money we earned from our hauling services, we created an IT company which we named SALVATOR Connection Resource, Inc.

SALVATOR is a Latin word for Redeemer or Savior. Salvator because we specialize in products and services related to security and network solutions, devices that will secure and save lives and properties.

Connection Resource, because our network solutions will bridge network connections.

This we think, is something that we are good at.

SALVATOR Connection Resource, Inc. has been until now serving clients nationwide.

If you don't know the pros and cons of starting a business, do not fret. You can always learn. Knowledge can be acquired.

Please see APPENDIX B for the different types of business organizations in the Philippines, and the different procedures of its registration. You can register your business by yourself. Just follow the instructions provided.

If you've acquired enough funds already, get help from a lawyer or a legal consultant to organize and set up your business properly.

Focus on your "bread and butter".

Knowing how to sell your products and services is the "bread and butter" of your business.

So what are you good at?

Is it sports, entertainment, dresses, accessories, cars, planning, events, computers, engineering, etc.? Whatever that is, you can always make money out of it. Be creative. Learn. Read.

Sometimes, you will not know how good you are at one thing until you are forced to do it. Don't be afraid to try out new things. Just don't break any law nor oppress anyone.

The next time you encounter a task and you find it extremely challenging, don't cower down, be courageous. Pull out all the courage you can muster, and do your best. Who knows that exact gigantic challenge will unleash the David in you.

Seize every opportunity. Don't be lazy, you might miss your chance. Always push yourself to your limits. God will help those who help themselves.

There are millions of people in the world. Only a few are entrepreneurs. The rest are employees, working for the entrepreneurs. Why is it so?

Mark Zuckerberg is GOOD AT COMPUTERS which led him to develop a social networking website (Facebook) that changed the world forever. Now he's a young billionaire and have helped a lot of people through his charity works.

David M. Consunji the founder and Chairman Emeritus of DMCI Holdings, Incorporated. He is a CIVIL ENGINEERING GRADUATE FROM UNIVERSITY OF THE PHILIPPINES – DILIMAN.

He started his construction business in 1954 as nothing more than a small contractor. Being a civil engineer, he must be good at what he is doing, construction business. Today, DMCI Holdings, Inc. is one of the country's top companies, helping Consunji become the 7th richest man in the Philippines.

Henry Sy, a Chinese-Filipino business magnate, successful investor, and philanthropist. He started out his career with a simple but friendly sari-sari store (neighborhood variety store), before going on to make a shoe retail store. Chairman of SM Prime Holdings Inc., the holding corporation for all his interests within his dominant empire.

Henry Sy has gone through much adversity in his life. He did not get success once and roll with it continuously; he had his ups and downs like many of us do. But what made him different and eventually earned him the success, is that **HE NEVER GAVE UP ON**

PURSUING HIS DREAMS. His success and achievements are not handed down on a silver platter, but earned through HARD WORK, PERSEVERANCE, MEETING THE RIGHT PEOPLE AT THE RIGHT TIME, the trials of life and through the will and determination to see things through to the end.

Just like Henry Sy, you might not be good at something specific, but if you have the right attitude, you can achieve anything.

On the other hand, if you are good at something, like Mark Zuckerberg and DMCI, and you work hard and persevere, success is guaranteed.

Zuckerberg have something special, something he is good at, that he converted into a multi-billion business. Who knows, you could be like him. You could have that talent, that something you are good at, that needs releasing and converted into a multi-billion business.

Chapter 3

What is your WHY?

I do not dream of becoming super wealthy. Having the comforts of life and a little extra, to help others, will do.

In the previous chapter, I mentioned that I dream of becoming a lawyer. When I was still in law school, my primary purpose of becoming an entrepreneur is to earn more money to support my living expenses and my school expenses.

Other than that, I also got tired of having bosses and company rules that restrict my freedom to use my talents, skills and ideas. I want to be my own boss and experiment on trying new ideas.

True enough, I was able to graduate from law school through the help of my businesses.

Because of the small successes we experienced, we got overwhelmed and hired many employees.

But those we hired were mostly fresh graduates, who still need more training and experience before becoming a positive contributor to the company.

Because of that, the company's cash flow went downhill, while the expenses were shooting up.

We reached to a point where we borrowed money for our operating expenses. Projects didn't materialize. Debts bloated. The company is becoming insolvent.

We failed to protect the most basic and important factor of staying in business. **Sales and Cash flow.**

We struggled to remain liquid, and we kept on borrowing money. Later did we know that we were already drowning in debts.

We were so reckless.

As we can no longer pay our sales team, if they will stay a little bit longer, we helped them find employment somewhere else.

We narrowed down our workforce and retained only the technical personnel.

We stayed in business despite the absence of a sales team, banking only on our existing clients for repeat purchases.

In business a stumble might prevent a fall. If we did not do what we did, we could have closed shop.

Our **WHY** originally was, "to provide products and services to our clients with agility and responsiveness that other big companies cannot provide due to their lengthy standard processes that our clients thought to be ridiculous".

It turned into "keep operating for the sake of our loyal clients who never left us and who has been good to us through the years."

What pushed you to do the things you do?

Vision.

How do you see yourself ten (10) years from now? Common question of an interviewer during job interviews.

Why is it important to have a vision?

An entrepreneur's life is full of challenges. You will eat challenges for breakfast, lunch and dinner, with small fragments in between for "merienda". In short, you live to solve problems, day in and day out.

If you don't have a vision, a dream that you look forward to, you will not be motivated to endure.

You don't solve problems for nothing.

An entrepreneur sacrifices his/her two (2) years to ten (10) years or more, in the hope of a lifetime of comfort. Because there is no such thing as an overnight success. Everything should be worked on and worked out.

Body builders go to the gym, to pump their muscles daily until they get a perfectly sculpted body.

Same thing with entrepreneurs. The daily challenges will develop your entrepreneurial muscles.

Do not dread problems, do not fear difficulties, because the lesson you learn from them now, will be your weapon in the future.

Your vision is a holistic picture of your dream. What you want for your business, for your personal life, or in your family life after you accomplished your goals.

Your goals are the things that you need to accomplish daily, weekly, monthly, or yearly in order to realize your vision. Small tasks that you need to accomplish in a short period of time, which should be SMART, Specific, Measurable, Attainable, Realistic, and Time-bounded.

Business crisis may push you to adjust your vision. If you are finally acquainted with the pros and cons of your industry, you might be compelled to change, modify, and alter the structure, mission and vision for your business.

Nevertheless, always resolve for the fulfillment of your vision.

"To be my own boss"

Common answer of an employee-turned-entrepreneur, who left his/her day job to start his/her own business.

If you are like this, sorry to rain on your parade, but being your own boss is ten times (10x) more difficult than being an employee who only focused on performing the task stated on his/her job description.

Employees do not worry about:

- the profitability of the business.
- the mounting expenses
- the bills
- the salaries
- the delayed collections.
- the taxes, permits and government regulations.
- the problem employees

All the employees worry about are his/her:

- KPIs
- Promotion
- 15/30
- Outfits for Christmas parties, General Assembly, outing etc.
- 13th month pay
- Bonuses
- Incentives

Being your own boss is not a walk in the park.

Yes, being "the boss" is cool. You get to do the things you want, the way you like it. You decide for yourself, and you don't need someone else's permission.

If you have employees, you have people under you, calling you Boss, Sir, Ma'am. But these people don't call you such for nothing.

They are your responsibility. You need to take care of their welfare as employees. It means accountability, expenses, and possible lawsuit if you messed up.

Employees are supposed to be assets, but they can be a liability sometimes. They can make or break your business.

There are grateful employees, and ungrateful ones. Nevertheless, whatever they are, it is your responsibility to treat them equally, justly, and fairly.

"To have more comforts in life"

If this is your "WHY", hold on to your seat...

BEING AND ENTREPRENEUR IS GENERALLY NOT COMFORTABLE.

The only comfort I could think of is, "you own your time".

It is also convenient to have employees working for you, instead of you personally do it yourself.

The rest is all inconvenienced.

But, if you are comfortable with inconveniences, this "WHY" is for you.

When I say inconvenience, did I already say that when we were just starting up, we slept like babies at night? We woke up every hour and cry? Asking and praying for God's guidance on how to solve the pressing problems waiting for us the next day?

These challenges include, bills that are due; salary; products that are still not available, but were needed yesterday; client pressure; government compliance that requires money to move, but funds is still not available; employees cheating on attendance; employees embezzling company funds; employees not showing up on the site and cause delays in the project; clients not paying on time; and so on...

When you are an entrepreneur, your only draw comfort from God's providence. That is why most entrepreneurs are devotees, because challenges toughen their faith.

"To exercise my own creativity without restrictions"

This is one of my WHYs. As I have mentioned in the preceding chapters, I was restricted to sell and offer certain products, when I was still an employee.

One time, I was presenting a project update, involving routers and network cabling with one of the biggest international hotel chains in Makati, during a business review, my boss rebuked me. He did that in front of all my colleagues. There were about twenty (20) of us. According to him, he has not authorized me to position those products and services.

I defended myself by saying, "Boss, the last time I checked, network routers were one of the products listed in our portfolio. I don't understand why I can't offer it to my clients".

He responded, "because I did not authorize you, that's all".

I find his actuations whimsical. Imagine, "just because he said so". Despite the fact that it is listed in our Product Portfolio.

I got tired of it, I resigned and open my own business where I offered Network and Security Solutions, the exact same products and services that my previous boss forbade me to sell.

When you have employees, it is imperative that you listen to them. They are personally interacting with the clients and they know very well, the situation out there. They can be a reliable source of business information and opportunities that your organization may benefit from.

"To secure my future, or my family's future"

This is also one of my WHYs. My parents used to tell me "Study well. We don't have anything to pass on to you but education".

"It is better to suffer now while you are still studying, than suffer poverty in the future."

I agree.

Yes, suffer now, enjoy later.

It is better to suffer the adversities now while building your money machine (business), and reap the fruits of your labor when you're older. Than to chill and relax now, but suffer the insufficiencies in the future.

It is better to struggle now and suffer the harshness of curing your ignorance, than remain ignorant forever.

It is better to start today, while you are still younger, stronger, and more resilient, than suffer when you're older and frail.

If you are failing now, it's okay. Some businesses, stabilize in two (2) years' time, but most businesses, stabilize in ten (10) years' time, or more.

Are you willing to suffer now, for the future happiness and convenience of your family?

Are you willing to suffer now, for a more comfortable future?

If what you are suffering for is better than what you have right now, it is worth it.

Chapter 4

Are you humble enough?

When I was still an employee, my job involves face to face interaction with clients. Because of that, it was always my priority to invest in my physical appearance.

Every payday it was my primary goal to doll myself up. So most of my money was invested in that area.

On the other hand, I also wanted to become a lawyer, so I would distribute funds between my school expenses and physical appearance on top of my bills. It was really difficult as I was juggling between law school and my demanding job. It was like being in between a rock and a hard place.

Time was such a scarce commodity as well. I didn't have the luxury of time to sleep eight (8) hours a day. My work starts at 8:30 am and ends at 6:30 pm. My classes start at 7:00pm and ends at 9:00 pm daily.

After class, I go home immediately to start reading my assignments for the next day until 2:00 in the morning. If there were lots of assigned cases which I can't finish reading until 2:00 am, I have to extend until 4:00am. Giving myself only two (2) hours of sleep as I need to wake up at 6:00 am to prepare for work.

I didn't have the luxury of time to go out with my friends.

While my friends and officemates were busy enjoying at the bar, I was at home burning the midnight oil. A typical thing for all law-students.

In my mind, I convinced myself that those sacrifices were just temporary, and that time will come that I can also enjoy, have a good time, and get enough rest. In the meantime, I need to endure.

Sacrifice is giving up something for the sake of a better cause. Time, sleep, gratification, anything that can be put off for the benefit of a greater reward.

In business, you will have to sacrifice so much time, energy and effort. And sometimes these sacrifices won't guarantee sure returns.

No matter how much time, money and energy you invested, it will not work as expected sometimes. And when it happens, there will be no one to turn to but yourself.

Because you want to be your own boss, you will also be on your own. In case you messed up, you cannot turn to anyone, you cannot point fingers and blame someone else. You will just humbly accept that you fail and vow to do better next time.

Conversely, if you succeed, you will get the benefits all by yourself. But it will not come easy. You will have to suffer.

Life is full of struggles, you will surely struggle in whatever kind of life you are leading. Make sure that your struggles count.

If you will just struggle, might as well struggle for something worthwhile. If you struggle in your day job, and you keep on complaining because it is not giving you the salary and the treatment you deserved based on the services you render, might as well leave that company and struggle for yourself.

I know a lot of people who keep on complaining about how cruel their bosses are. How scanty their salaries compare to the service they've rendered, but they did not leave. They're so afraid to try new things, yet complains incessantly.

If you are this type of person, you need to really reconfigure your outlook. In the long run, your health will suffer. You are willing to risk your health for someone else, yet you don't risk for yourself.

The problem with society right now is that, they became fond of watching people achieving or failing. They're just contented of being mere spectators.

Today's digital age, where information is accessible at the tips of our fingers, it is easier to explore anything and get warned of its possible pitfalls.

However, due to the same accessibility of a lot of information, people became so lazy. They want things to just fall in their laps, to be spoon-fed to them. Most of us don't want to exert effort. We became so lazy.

Because of that, laziness were converted into a profitable business concept. See, for example, Globe Gcash, LalaMove, grocery delivery, Angkas, Lazada, Shoppee, other online stores, among others.

People no longer want to leave their houses, or their offices. And these brilliant entrepreneurs found a way to profit from the situation.

If people are lazy, you work hard.

That means giving up comfort and convenience, to wipe someone else's butt.

Sometimes the road less traveled, is less traveled for a reason - Jerry Seinfield

"Life is difficult. This is a great truth, one of the greatest truths. It is a great truth because once we truly see this truth, we transcend it. Once we truly know that life is difficult - once we truly understand and accept it - then life is no longer difficult. Because once it is accepted, the fact that life is difficult no longer matters." - M. Scott Peck

Education is one thing.

Education doesn't only mean academic degrees, it is most importantly life education.

I know some friends who are graduates of Law, bar passers, but are jobless. One even went abroad to work as a helper. They are well educated academically, but not practically.

On the other hand, I know some friends who did not finish college, but own businesses that are profitable.

Your academic degrees will train you how to become good employees, but your life experiences will help you become better employers. If you have both, there is no doubt that you are capable of building a business empire.

Attitude is everything.

Pride, entitlement, laziness, lack of discipline among others, destroy a person.

If you are not willing to suffer humiliation, you are doomed to fail.

"For those who exalt themselves will be humbled, and those who humble themselves will be exalted." - Matthew 23:12

Why do you think there are lots of road rage?

These are people who don't want to be stepped on. No one wants to be second. All of them, those who are involved in road rage, want to be first. No one is willing to let go of his pride and swallow his ego. No one wants to humble himself.

If you become an entrepreneur, aside from eating challenges for breakfast, lunch and dinner, you also swallow your ego for dessert.

You cannot always be right. Even if you are right, you cannot always exercise and invoke your right.

For example, your client's terms of payment is Fifteen (15) days after delivery. Before delivery, the client pressures you to deliver his/her orders on time. Because you promised to deliver as agreed upon, you will do everything in your power to comply.

Now it's your turn to collect payment after Fifteen (15) days. However, the client asked for an extension as the signatory is still out of town.

In the given situation, you have all the right to compel your client to pay you on time as agreed upon in the contract, the way they pressured you to deliver on time.

But will you do it?

No. Because even if you are right, you need to swallow your ego; you have to show understanding, and cut the client some slack.

It is like following an unwritten law that states that "only clients are allowed to pressure the vendor, never the other way around". The reason is goodwill.

It is better to maintain goodwill with your clients, than to lose them to your competitors.

However, there are also clients who will take advantage of you. Those types who will only get your products and services, but when it comes to payment, they will do everything in their power to evade.

This one is contemptible. This is common when you offer services payable in progress billing. Their modus operandi is to render your progress inadequate for the payment that you billed them.

It is unfair to the vendor as the client's payment is dependent on the bias assessment of their assigned assessor, who was specifically instructed to assess the progress based on what they can only pay at the moment.

Not all clients are like this. There are a few who stays true to their business obligation, and treats their vendors fairly and justly.

Entrepreneurs suffer mentally, emotionally, and physically. It is sometimes very exhausting that it depletes your energy.

But if you are wise, you can let it go. After all, nothing belongs to you. They are all God's.

Yes, you worked hard for it, and you did everything to have it, but after all is said and done and it is still not working in your favor, you just have to let it go.

Be sure to keep a heart like Job's, who always proclaim the name of the Lord, no matter his situation. Be it good or Bad, it is only the Lord, who decides which belongs to whom. Who are we to question His will?

Nevertheless, it does not mean that you will be complacent. In case you find yourself in a situation wherein you need to protect your right, by all means hire a lawyer. As soon as you've done everything to fight for your right, let go and let God. In this way, you will be at peace.

Chapter 5

What will stop you?

Drawbacks, distress, and the crisis may handicapped you. Financial constrains, the pressure, the constant pounding of problems will make you look for a steady paycheck.

When you want to be an entrepreneur, be prepared to suffer. There will be no steady paycheck that comes in every month to pay for your expenses. Most especially if your clients don't pay on time, thereby putting you in a tight situation which will push you to look for funds from other sources.

Employees may not deliver what is expected of them, in this manner they become liabilities instead of assets.

Suppliers may hound as you can't pay them on time because the funds are still not available.

Clients do not pay on time. The worst part is that you cannot pressure your clients to pay you the same way your supplier puts pressure on you, thus, making you resort to borrowing money again from other sources. You are now buried in debts.

These are just some of the tough moments in an entrepreneur's life, most especially if you are running a start-up business.

You are responsible for all the areas of your business from the bottom line, your sales, to your employees and suppliers. Whatever happens, you will be accountable. You cannot pass on the hat to someone else. It is just you, every bit of it yourself.

You will sleep like a baby, that means waking up in the middle of the night to cry.

These things will make you stop.

It happened to us. We downsized our workforce, retaining only 3 persons just to survive. We became insolvent, we can no longer pay for our car mortgage, our house mortgage. We reached to a point wherein we no longer even buy food, as we need to prioritize our employees' salaries.

It came to a point that I decided to seek employment again for the sake of having a steady paycheck.

But when I saw the salary package they offered me apropos the job description, I can't help but think that it is still better to work for my own company and earn the same or greater, in my own time and pace.

Desperate moment calls for desperate action.

Once you have tried being an entrepreneur, you no longer want to go back to work for someone else again.

Running your own business is a gamble. There is no guarantee that you will win.

Since you don't have a steady paycheck, and your income comes from the business that you manage, a time will come that your funds will be depleted and you will be penniless.

During this time, you will start second guessing your abilities. Questioning your worth.

You will even ask yourself if you are good at anything at all. Your self-esteem shrinks down and you begin to sulk and withdraw from people.

These things will make you give up.

When this happens, help yourself.

There are several business books out there such as this, detailing some of the greatest entrepreneur successes and struggles that will help you overcome failure, frustrations, and depression. Understand that you are not alone; that you are not a failure; that you can still recover.

Entrepreneurship is not for everyone. It is only for those who are tough enough to handle stress.

That is why entrepreneurs should have:

MENTAL TOUGHNESS

and

EMOTIONAL INTELLIGENCE

These two (2) should go hand in hand. There are various ways to acquire these aptitudes. I for one enrolled in karate to develop my mental toughness and emotional intelligence.

I lost both my parents to a heart problem, and my brother at age Forty four (44) to a heart problem as well. So I made up a covenant with myself to stay healthy and never succumb to a heart problem like them.

I kept on reading self-help books about mental toughness as I believe that heart problems are sometimes caused by poor emotional intelligence, and mental weakness.

Mark Divine in his book, "The way of the SEAL", said, that Martial arts will give you the mental fitness of a warrior. It will teach you perseverance, patience, strengthen your will, your mental ability, aside from the fact that you will become more physically confident after learning how to defend yourself.

For that reason, I enrolled in Kyokushin Karate.

The training in Kyokushin karate is physically and mentally exhausting. And the "Kumite" (sparring) are really painful.

You will get hit in any parts of your body, to the point that you will get peeved, but you cannot allow yourself to get peeved because you will lose, not against the opponent but against yourself. That's when your emotional intelligence is being practiced.

You cannot also give up, because you are expected to persevere. You will not have a choice but to tell yourself to go on, to endure, despite the physical pain, despite the exhaustion. That's when your mental toughness is being developed.

If you are an entrepreneur, you will need to cultivate a perfect blend of spiritual, physical, mental and emotional fitness, to prevent yourself from yielding to frustration and depression.

"Problems do not go away. They must be worked through, or else they remain, forever a barrier to the growth and development of the spirit" - Scott Peck

You cannot avoid life's problems. No matter what you do, whether you are an entrepreneur or not, you will have your own share of predicaments.

You cannot solve life's problems except by facing them and solving them.

So, when you are faced with so much tribulation in your business life, and you have had enough of it, it is understandable to abandon ship, and call it quits. But before you do that, look back, and ask yourself, "Why did I do this in the first place?"

There is no easy way, nor the other way, but to endure, withstand, and persist. You have to confront the issues, wrestle the helplessness, straighten the mess, and clear up the wreckage. There is no escaping it. Otherwise, it will just keep on recurring.

The ride might be bumpy for now, as you are journeying on an unpaved road, and no one will pave your way through it. You will have to do it yourself.

Big businesses started small. It also went through a whole lot of trouble before it became what it is today.

Take courage, if others can, why can't you?

The SM Story

Of Henry Sy – ShoeMart

"There is no such thing as overnight success or easy money. If you fail, do not be discouraged; try again. When you do well, do not change your ways. Success is not just good luck: it is a combination of hard work, good credit standing, opportunity, readiness and timing. Success will not last if you do not take care of it."- Henry Sy, Sr.

Shī ZhìChéng, (Henry's Chinese name), was born on December 25, 1923, to an <u>impoverished family</u> in Jinjiang, a town near Xiamen, China. The entire family left China for good in 1936, so they could be with their family patriarch who was then a proprietor of a thriving variety store in Manila.

Henry remembers having to <u>clear the store's counter, which served as his sleeping place</u>, after helping his father run the store for 12 hours.

Unfortunately, World War II came and their family store was burned down; but the war's aftermath gave him the opportunity to earn income by buying and selling post war goods including the shoes of some enterprising G.I. Joes.

The success of the shoe-peddling business later gave the young man from Jinjiang, China, the idea of opening his own shoe store.

This was how Henry Sy, Sr. came to be the founder of the Philippine's largest retailing company known as **SM**.

The acronym stands for Shoe Mart, the name of the small shoe store business he started in 1958 at the "Avenida", which was Manila's most popular commercial district during the post war era.

Initially, however, the young businessman encountered <u>difficulties in finding a local shoe manufacturer who would cooperate with his ideas on the kind of shoes to sell.</u>

He was quite determined and confident in pursuing his plans because they were mostly based on his own research. He continuously learned from his customers, his employees, and his suppliers and practically studied the growing needs of the Philippine market.

Henry never lost sight of his goals even as he succeeded with his shoe store venture; he <u>pursued a college degree</u> in one of Manila's top universities, because education for Henry was a means to learn more ways on how to augment his income.

Today, after more than 50 years, the shoe store has evolved into becoming a network of 44 large-scale shopping malls not only in the Philippines but throughout Asia and lays claim to three of the world's top ten shopping centers: the **SM** City-North **EDSA** (ranked 3rd), the **SM** Mall of Asia (ranked 4th) and **SM** MegaMall (ranked 7th), which are all located in the Philippines.

The malls have become typical destinations for family weekend recreation and leisure, regardless of social stature, since the stores are strategically scattered throughout the country.

Henry Sy, Sr. was listed by Forbes in its 2010 edition as the richest man in the Philippines and was honored by the prestigious magazine in 2009 for being one of the Filipino Heroes of Philanthropy.

Through the SM Foundation, solutions to social problems of health, education and spiritual assistance have been extended to people in remote areas, by way of mobile health and dental clinics, scholarship awards, and contributions for building public schools, Catholic chapels and youth centers.

Reference: brighthub.com

The JOLLIBEE Story

Of Tony Tan Caktiong, Jollibee

"Twenty-seven years ago we didn't have a firm vision that we would be number one, but we had a rough vision that we would go outside the Philippines. We also had a goal: to take care of our customers and employees and to enjoy what we're doing. Once we did all these things, the profits would come." Tony Tan Caktiong

Tony Tan Caktiong was born on October 07, 1960 to a working-class family from Fujian, China, who migrated to the Philippines during the post WWII era.

Tony's father found <u>work as a cook</u> at a Buddhist temple in downtown Manila and accordingly <u>scrimped and saved</u> so he could open his own Chinese restaurant in order to provide for his family.

His father's hard work and perseverance made it possible for Tony Tan Caktiong to earn a BS in Chemical Engineering at the University of Sto. Tomas, the Philippine's oldest university.

In 1975, Tony ventured into the food business by buying an ice cream parlor franchise from the once famous Magnolia Ice Cream House.

<u>The parlor was small and nondescript,</u> which catered mostly to the well heeled shoppers of Cubao. They were customers who could afford to buy cleverly concocted, but rather expensive cobblers, floats, milkshakes, banana splits, sundaes and parfaits.

However, most of Tony's regulars wished that the parlor had something else to offer, other than ice-cream concoctions. Hence, the small, nondescript store started offering sandwiches, fries and fried chicken, which started to attract the attention of other tired and hungry shoppers, movie-theater goers and passers-by.

The word fast food was still unheard of at that time, but it was what the small store had to offer at affordable prices.

Soon after, customers started filling the store beyond its capacity as they patiently waited for their turn to be served. By 1978, Tony added six more ice cream parlors around Metro Manila, but the ice cream treats were no longer the attraction.

Taking inspiration from America's fast-rising McDonald's food chain, Tony and his family decided to transform the ice cream parlors into fast food outlets.

They strategized with their new venture by coming up with a unique name and symbol. Since Tony personally felt happy by working busily as a bee to produce honey, which in Tony's case was money, he and his family decided to work on the busy bee concept.

Hence, they came up with the large red and yellow bee with an effervescent smile on its face and called it "Jollibee".

The once nondescript ice cream kiosk became Jollibee Food Corporation and braved the arrival of the McDonald's fast food chain in the Philippines in 1981. Jollibee came out unscathed as it became the first Philippine food chain to break the one billion peso sales mark in 1989.

The groundwork for global expansion was laid out when it became the first food service company to be listed in the Philippine Stock Exchange, in which capitalization funds started pouring in.

The rest is history, as Jollibee now owns its former competitors in the local fast food chain business, Greenwich Pizza, Chowking (oriental dishes), Red

Ribbon and DeliFrance bakeshops and lately Mang Inasal (chicken specialty house). Today, these fast food chains are found in different parts of the world along with Jollibee's globally recognized trade name.

Tony's management and leadership style garnered the recognition not only of the Philippine's local award-giving bodies, but also that of the "World Entrepreneur Award in 2004, in Monte Carlo, Monaco" He is the first Filipino entrepreneur to receive the prestigious award.

In return, Jollibee Foundation was established in 2005, to specifically address the social responsibility of the company.

The foundation provides assistance to its employees and communities on a nationwide scale regarding matters of education, housing, leadership and social developments, environmental conservation and responses to disaster problems in times of calamitous events.

*Reference: brighthub.com

The HAPEE toothpaste Story

of Cecilio K. Pedro, Lamoiyan Corporation

"Fighting multinationals was very tough. At first, everyone thought I was crazy. They told me, how will I

survive this? True enough, it's by the grace of God that I'm still here in the toothpaste industry after 20 years. God is good," – Cecilio K. Pedro

Cecilio K. Pedro is a Filipino businessman of Chinese descent, but his story is not the typical rags-to-riches tale but about turning adversity into triumph.

He once headed Aluminum Container, Inc. which was the major supplier of the collapsible aluminum toothpaste tubes that were formerly used by local manufacturers of Colgate-Palmolive, Procter and Gamble and the Philippine Refining Company (now Unilever).

However, technological innovations and the environmental concerns over aluminum materials prompted the multinational companies to make use of the plastic-laminated toothpaste tubes as an alternative.

As a result, <u>Cecilio's aluminum factory closed shop in 1985</u>, but this didn't stop him from exploring other ways to put his factory equipment into good use.

Cecilio decided to compete with the multinational giants by producing locally made toothpastes and hit them where it would hurt the most — the selling price.

He founded the Lamoiyan Corporation, which became the manufacturer of the first locally produced toothpastes "Hapee" and "Kutitap" (sparkle). They were sold in the Philippine market at 50 percent lower than the selling price of the well known foreign brands.

Although Colgate countered by dropping the price of its toothpaste products 20 percent lower than their original price, Cecilio Pedro came up with another innovation that gave him a further edge in the local market scene.

He developed multi-flavored toothpastes for children that came brightly packaged in tubes and boxes adorned with "Sesame Street" characters.

Today, the market for the budget-friendly toothpaste brands has expanded to neighboring countries like China, Vietnam and Indonesia.

The low-priced toothpaste was not the only strategy that took Lamoiyan Corporation to the pinnacles of success. The company was lauded for having the "Most Outstanding Program for Equal Employment Opportunity" by providing work opportunities to the country's hearing-impaired community members.

Reference: brighthub.com

The ZEST-O JUICE DRINKS Story

of Alfredo Yao, Zest-O Corporation.

"When Zest-O was established, it had a single yet valuable mission, to provide products with immense consumer value and quality that exceeds even the scrutiny of global measure." Alfredo Yao

Alfredo Yao's story is yet another rags-to-riches tale of a self-made businessman who rose from poverty through hard work and determination.

He had to face life's hard realities at the age of 12 when his father died; his mother tried to support Alfredo and five other siblings with her earnings as a sidewalk vendor.

Through the help of a relative, he was able to finish his elementary and high school education.

However, he was unable to complete his college education at the Mapua Institute of Technology, which he attended while doing odd jobs at a warehouse of a packaging company.

Through a cousin who was working with a printing press, Alfredo Yao learned the ropes on printing cellophane wrappers for candies and biscuits and went on to venture into operating a printing press business.

The business thrived for about 20 years until Alfredo Yao saw the potentials of the "doy packs", then the latest European packaging technology. Initially, Alfredo's first intention was to offer the "doy-pack" packaging to some local juice manufacturers, but since there were no takers, he ventured into the juice manufacturing business himself.

In 1980, Alfredo Yao started concocting fruit juices in his own kitchen and launched the Zest-O orange drinks in the same year. It became an instant hit as every mother saw the practicality of putting the light but tightly-packed orange drinks in their kids' lunch boxes.

Kids loved it that their chilled fruit drinks stayed cold and fresh till snack time.

Today, Zest-O drinks come in 12 variants and command 80% of the market for fruit juices. It has expanded its business in China, Australia, New Zealand, Korea, Singapore, the U.S. and Europe and has helped revitalize the fruit growing industry in the provinces, particularly the Philippine's native orange variety called "dalandan".

The doy packs are being recycled by local cottage industries into handbags and are now being exported to other countries.

Aside from expanding the business by producing other ready-to-eat and ready-to-cook food products, Zest-O Corporation now owns the former Asian Spirit Airlines, which CEO Alfredo Yao aptly renamed as Zest Air.

Reference: brighthub.com

The NATIONAL BOOKSTORE Story

of Soccoro C. Ramos, National Bookstore.

"You have to adjust to the flow of business. If you're not open to change, your business can't move on." – Socorro Ramos

The matriarch of National Book Store, the Philippine's largest chain of bookstores, which retails not only all types of books, but also greeting cards, office supplies and craft materials, was born as Socorro Cancio on September 23,1923 in Sta. Cruz, Laguna.

Socorro's mother brought her and her elder siblings to Manila when she was ten years old. Her elder sisters helped augment the family income by working in a candy and bubble gum factory.

The young girl, however, was able to get <u>odd jobs during summer by peeling off the paper of discarded cigarettes for recycling purposes,</u> and she was paid five centavos for every pack of cigarette given to her.

At the age of 18, her brother married one of the children of an established bookstore owner in Manila; hence, she was able to <u>land a job as a salesgirl in one of its stalls.</u>

There Socorro met Jose, the son of the bookstore clan, who was to become her husband. However, it was a relationship that her parents forbade. Technically, Socorro's brother and Jose were related as in-laws, which made Socorro and Jose's love affair seemingly improper.

The young lass was sent back to Laguna in order to cut short the affair, but the strong-willed Socorro went back to Manila on her own and married Jose.

The young couple braved their parents' anger, which eventually died down when Socorro's firstborns were twins. Jose took over a branch of his family's bookstore, which he and Socorro renamed National Book Store.

As if fate was against them, World War II struck and the Japanese occupation prevented them from selling most of their books, since they were often regarded as questionable.

The war raged on and their bookstore was destroyed when Manila was declared an "open city" to America's bombing attacks in order to drive away Japan's Imperial Army.

The post-war era saw the couple relocating their National Book Store to "Avenida", which worked out well because business started picking up in no time at all.

Three years later, a storm tore off the roof of their establishment, which left them with nothing but worthless goods to sell.

The couple didn't give up, but instead tried to rebuild from scratch once again. This time they had a more definite goal.

Every cent earned by the business was used to pay for a nine-story building, where the first official National Book Store was located.

Socorro Ramos's hands-on approach in negotiating with local and foreign publishers as well as suppliers gave the bookstore its low purchasing and low-selling power.

She became acquainted with writers, book lovers and other personalities who could provide her with information about the changing times.

After several decades, National Book Store has become an institution with 108 branches dispersed throughout the country.

Through the company's foundation, they have provided assistance to the underserved sectors of different communities by way of a mobile library, which brings books and school supplies for different socio-civic donation programs.

Reference: brighthub.com

The MERCURY DRUGSTORE Story

Of Mariano Que, Mercury Drugstore

Mariano Que initially <u>worked as an employee of a drugstore during the prewar era,</u> but like most typical successful entrepreneurs, Que found his opportunities after the war and during the advent of the American occupation.

The destruction of the prewar establishments left everyone starting and rebuilding from scratch, and those who had a wider perception of the people's needs seemed to had the greater advantage.

Mariano Que saw the demand for sulfa drugs, since most of the Philippine pharmacies hardly had enough resources to go by.

Using his prewar experience as a drugstore employee, <u>Mariano invested in 100 pesos worth of sulfathiazole tablets and peddled them in single doses so they could be affordable to the poverty-stricken sector.</u>

He rolled over his profits until he had enough money to build a wooden pushcart. That way, he could peddle a wider assortment of pharmaceutical products.

Other peddlers imitated his marketing and selling strategy, but Que made a difference. He had a reputation for selling only quality and unexpired medical products, and soon enough he had a steady clientele.

By 1945, Mariano had saved enough resources, which enabled him to set up his first store, aptly called Mercury Drug. The Roman god Mercury carried the caduceus symbol, which was largely associated with the medical profession.

Despite the store's establishment, Mariano invested in motorized vehicles in order to provide drug delivery services to his valued customers. He also expanded his store hours to 17 hours a day, 7 days a week, since he recognized that the need for medication may come unexpectedly.

In 1952, the stores were open 24/7, which made the drugstore become a valuable part of the community.

In 1960, the Ayala Group of Companies offered Mariano Que a space to lease in the shopping center that was about to be developed in the heart of Makati. Thus, the second Mercury Drug opened, this time as a self-service pharmacy.

The rest is a history of more innovations and technological adoption of computer-guided controls and biological refrigerators.

These improvements allowed the drugstore's expansion into other life-saving medications. The new branches of today are superstores as they carry more than just medicines, but other consumer products from food to household for health and beauty items.

Mercury Drug created a reputation that every Filipino household could rely on; and there was a store in nearly every town and city across the country.

Today, there are about 700 Mercury stores, some of which are under franchise.

All these fulfilled Mariano Que's goal of making safe medication available and accessible to every Filipino community.

Today, Mariano's daughter, Vivian Que Azcona, continues to uphold his company's visions and missions. In return for their customers' unwavering loyalty, Mercury Drug celebrates their annual anniversaries by holding a free clinic to the indigent, for which the appropriate medications for their illnesses are likewise given for free.

Reference: brighthub.com

The CDO FOODSPHERE Story

Of Corazon D. Ong, CDO Foodsphere, Inc.

Corazon D. Ong being a dietitian by profession who used her knowledge to create affordable processed meat products that could <u>compete with the already well known and established processed meat brands.</u>

Initially, it was only a hobby where she could put to good use her creativity and skill in the culinary arts. She came up with corned beef, hotdogs, meatloaf, hamburger patties and ham, an entity that she later sold as a home business.

She founded CDO Foodsphere in 1975; as the product's reputation for affordable quality became widespread, the demand for CDO products likewise increased.

The creative homemaker understood every mother's need for quick lunch fixes for their children, but convenience should also come in affordable packages.

Corazon likewise understood the taste preferences of Filipino children but her knowledge of ingredients and their nutritional values gave her product the advantage.

Today, CDO Foodsphere is a highly-recognized supplier of meat toppings for Yum! Restaurant International, a known operator of global Quick Service

Restaurants (QSR), which includes Pizza Hut, KFC, Taco Bell and Long John Silver.

Locally, CDO supplies the meat toppings to nine out of ten QSRs operating in the Philippines. The clamor for CDO products stems from numerous awards and recognitions that the processed meat products have received, owing to their quality and excellence.

Reference: brighthub.com

The LACTOPAFI Story

Of Engineer Gregorio G. Sanchez, Jr., Lactopafi probiotic supplement

Gregorio G. Sanchez, Jr. is a civil engineer by profession formerly engaged in civil construction works. He served as a Provincial Board Member in Cebu City, where one of his concerns was the malnutrition among the pigs being raised.

On his own, <u>he went into research and performed experiments using only pots and pans and a small tank as his equipment.</u> His persistence finally led to the development of a food supplement that would smother the bad bacteria in livestock, which he called "LactoPAFI Probiotic Bacteria.

The success of the probiotic bacteria developed by Engineer Sanchez later on gained global recognition as a superior bacterial strain for its ability to restore good bacteria to the body. This gave the engineer greater confidence in developing a health drink (LactoVitale) and personal care products like soaps, shampoos and toothpastes with LactoPAFI as an important ingredient.

As a result, his LactoPAFI products are now being exported to Norway, France, Australia, New Zealand, Hong Kong, Japan and the U.S. The US FDA issued its approval of the product in 2005 while locally garnering recognition for product excellence from different award giving bodies.

Reference: brighthub.com

The SPI TECHNOLOGIES INC. Story

Of Ernest L. Cu, CFW Information Services call center workstation

Ernest L. Cu <u>transformed a simple data entry service company into becoming one of the country's largest outsourcing service providers</u>.

His company's core business sources are mostly contracts for generating projects, which involve customer service relationships and IT services. The CRM services became quite successful, which spurred the growth of telemarketing services.

The demand led to the establishment of the first call center in the Philippines in 1999, which was initially called as "e Telecare International".

The center is largely focused on providing U.S.companies' outsourcing needs. The call center company later changed its name to eTelecare Global Soltions in 2004.

Cu's company greatly values the services of the human resources behind his company; hence he acknowledges that his most immediate social responsibility is to provide a lucrative source of livelihood to its more than 6,000 employees and their respective families.

*Reference: brighthub.com

The COMPUTER CHIPS Story

Of Diosdado Banatao, Computer Chips

Diosdado Banatao was <u>born to a rice farmer in an upland farming barrio</u> in Cagayan Valley and to a plain housewife; hence, one would have hardly envisioned him as a Filipino version of Bill Gates.

As a child, he used to <u>walk barefoot just so he could acquire an elementary and high school education</u>. Determined to pursue a college education, he went to

Manila, took up electrical engineering and eventually graduated cum laude.

Due to his excellent academic performance, he was able to land a job as a pilot trainee of Philippine Airlines. This paved the way for a job offer as a design engineer coming from Boeing Co., which brought him to the U.S. Thereafter, he pursued and completed a Master's Degree in Electrical Engineering and Computer Science at Stanford University.

It was while working with some of the leading-edge technology companies that Diosdado Banatao had the opportunity to design the first single-chip 16-bit microprocessor-based calculator.

In 1981, the inventor Ethernet was looking for a more efficient method of linking computers and Diosdado was assigned by Seeq Technology to do the task. This was how Diosdado Banatao came to develop the single-chip controller that provided the data-link control and the transreceiver in the first 10-Mbit Ethernet CMOS.

Diosdado saw the opportunity of setting-up his own company by designing chip sets; in no time, he was able to raise $500,000 as seed capital to put up Monstroni 1985.

His company's determination paid off after they successfully developed the first system logic chip set that lowered the cost of building personal computers that were more powerful. He then went on to build another company called Chips and Technologies, which created another chips set for enhancing the so-called graphic adapter.

In less than a year, Diosdado's company realized sales of $12 million in the first quarter alone, thus creating a tremendous response from investors when the company went public.

In 1996, Diosdado sold the Chips and Technologies Co. to Intel for $430 million.

Diosdao Banatao went on to invest, oversee and sell companies by assuming the role of master investor and master capitalist.

In all these successes, Diosdado never forgot his roots and Filipino heritage. His "Banatao Filipino American Fund" provides assistance to Northern California students who are of Filipino heritage, to help them build a future by pursuing a college degree in engineering.

The elementary school, he attended in Cagayan Valley is the only public school in the region with the most modern computer system.

*Reference: brighthub.com

These great Filipino entrepreneurs worked their way through different challenges in order to succeed. They succeeded by keeping their sights focused on goals that are governed by the values of business ethics and social responsibility.

Chapter 6

How will I start?

Are you tired of being an employee?

Have you had enough of making other people rich, instead of making yourself rich?

If you are the type who is not afraid of trying new things, of taking risks, you surely have a chance of becoming a successful entrepreneur.

But if you are the type who only complains, but afraid of doing anything unfamiliar, afraid of the unknown, becoming an entrepreneur is not for you.

Don't get discouraged. Read on. Finish the book. Becoming an entrepreneur is not that hard. To start rolling, take the first step. And that is to know where to begin.

"We cannot solve our problems with the same thinking we used when we created them" Einstein.

"Your life doesn't get better by chance, It gets better by change" - Jim Rohn.

If we want something we've never had, we got to do something we've never done. Old ways won't open new doors.

Everyone wants to be something or somebody, but only some end up achieving it. Why?

They have the following:

- Strong Belief
- Integrity
- Intelligence / Knowledge of the craft
- Plan
- Discipline

Strong belief

At this age and time when faith in God becomes unpopular due to countless attacks from different views, organizations, sects, religions, agnostics, atheists, or just simply disinterested individuals, it became a bit harder to exercise and proclaim our faith.

Faith is vital.

By knowing that everything you possess are not yours, but God's, losing them won't hurt. For they are not yours in the first place.

If God grants you possessions, glorify Him. If He gives it to someone else, let His will be done, and still glorify Him.

It doesn't mean that you will just sit there and let others run the show.

"With great blessings, comes great responsibility." Familiar?

It is your duty to protect your blessings so it can serve its purpose. God entrusted them to you for a reason. Fortify them.

Use your God-given ability, knowledge and authority to identify sneaky thieves and fend off enemies.

Being the honored beneficiary of God's generosity, you are accountable for whatever happens to your business, employees, relationships, and every privileges and rights incidental thereto.

Do not worry. Worry won't take you anywhere. Do not join the worry-party of the enemy. Defeat worries by counting on the peace that comes from the Lord.

If God is for you, who can be against you?

You are covered, have faith!

Integrity

Integrity is doing the right thing even if no one is watching.

If you are honest in small things, you are honest with great things. If you can take care of small problems, you can take care of the big ones. What we actually perceived to be great or grand is just a collection of small intertwined matters. Big problems are just tiny unresolved matters partying together. Disturb their celebration, tear them apart. Solving those small matters, one by one, will slowly diminish its scale, and will be consequently dissolved.

A person loses confidence in someone, because of small neglected details. Small concerns can be a pain in the neck. If left unresolved, could ripen into a bigger mess and compromise relationships.

In dealing with customers, transparency is very important. They should be apprised of the scope of the job that you will render for them. To protect your interest, always reduced it in writing, detailing all the items, disclosing all cost, without hidden charges.

It is perfectly fine to impute reasonable mark-up, equivalent to the weight of the job contracted, or the product to be delivered, or services to be rendered. What the customers hate is dishonesty.

Customers don't like surprises, especially when it involves time and money. Such as delayed delivery and additional charges. Like most of us, they only like what is favorable to them.

Also, no matter how great your relationship with your customer is, only one mistake can expunge all your efforts and good reputation. And it would take time to bring those back again.

Intelligence / Knowledge of your craft

If you already know what you are good at, or have decided to focus on a certain craft, start working on it. Competition is fierce. Develop it further and have something significant and unique to offer.

Most businesses in your field may have already been offering the same package, pricing, convenience of use, features, benefits, etc., that you are now thinking about. Investigate further. You might uncover what the customers actually need.

What are customers' basic need?

o Fast service
o Approachable and kind personnel,
o Availability.
o Reasonable price

Most customers don't mind the cost, as long as, you deliver what they want.

Enroll in classes related to your chosen field. There are many short courses offered now online or within your locality that are searchable on the internet.

Local Government Units of the Philippines are conducting free trainings for their Livelihood Programs, involving sewing, soap making, polvoron making, etc.

They also provide free start-up kit/package such as, sewing machines, livestock, and others. Take advantage of the government programs, contact your local government officials to know more about it.

YouTube also provides a wide range of DO It Yourself (DIY) videos to learn from.

Our generation is the most fortunate when it comes to information accessibility. In this age and time, if you are industrious enough, you can be whatever you want to be. Acquiring knowledge is easy. But mere possession of knowledge is futile if not applied. Knowledge is NOT power. Applied Knowledge is power.

Get Certifications. Do not underestimate the power of a certificate. When competition is tight, it will be a written testimony of your capabilities. In project biddings, among competitors with equal capabilities, it is the qualifying factor.

Plan

If you fail to plan, you plan to fail, says one author.

If you always do things in the spur of the moment basis, depending on your whims and caprices, without proper planning, your chances of failing is high.

Whatever you are good at, think of ways to OFFER IT FOR A FEE.

If you are an accountant, there are small companies that look for a freelance or on-call accountants to help them in their mandatory financial reports and **BIR** compliance.

If you are an athlete, or you are good at dancing, or martial arts, create your own service package and offer it to schools, fitness centers, and gyms; or advertise your services on social media and do your sessions at the local parks or public plaza. You can collect payment in a per session basis.

If you are good at doing make-up, you can do a tutorial or offer your services at weddings, debut, birthdays, and other special occasions. You may partner with wedding coordinators and cameramen for a wider market.

If you are a teacher, and you're not a board passer yet, you can offer tutoring classes, online or in person.

If you are a musician, you can offer your services at weddings and parties, even online dubs. You may also accept tutoring classes.

If you are a carpenter and you are good at making furniture, fixtures and other woodworks, offer your works to villages, restaurants, condos, hotels, offices and other establishments where you think your products can be utilized.

The list goes on.

Whatever talents, skills, and expertise you possess, there are multiple ways of selling them.

You may start by doing the following:

1. Identify your target customers.

List down your prospects. Get their contact information.

Contact person:
Address:
Email Address:
Phone / Mobile Number:

Start your business without shelling out money. Look for clients who can trust you with a "full payment before delivery" payment scheme.

That is why integrity is very important. Invest in your reputation. People don't just entrust their money to anyone.

When we started our business, we only chose clients who can accept our standard Terms of Payment. If a client insists on an unfavorable payment scheme, we let them go. Of course, this changes over time. After few more transactions, when you can already afford, you may give them a more favorable terms.

You need to profile your prospects properly.

Trust me, there are still many customers out there who are willing to abide by your terms and conditions, provided that you can assure them that you can deliver exactly what they want; how they want it done; and when they want it delivered. Always a win-win situation.

2. Determine your business platform.

Are you going to offer your products and services online or at a physical store?

Offering your products and services online is much cheaper. The internet is a good marketing tool. Social media is free. There is only a small amount of premium required if you want to advertise to a broader market.

If you opt to acquire a physical store, or an office, you have to consider the operating costs, cost of construction if necessary, overhead, etc.

Position your business where it can be noticed and draw the most customers.

Legitimize your business. Have it duly registered. Check APPENDIX B for more information; or, ask a lawyer, or a legal consultant for help.

3. Formulate your product Portfolio.

A product portfolio is the collection of all the products or services you offer. Since you are just starting up, offer only what you can confidently deliver.

Do not over promise and under-deliver. "Value ads" look good on paper, but if you can't deliver it, it will ruin you. Let the client experience it instead.

It is better to delight a client with an unexpected value added benefits, than to disappoint him/her with false promises.

4. Determine the right pricing for your products or services.

Compare your pricing with that of your competitors' similar products and services. Make adjustments if needed.

To be competitive, do not be cheap that your customer might think you are of low quality, nor very expensive that you become a superfluity.

Again, best customers don't mind the cost as long as they are satisfied with what they get.

5. Identify your workforce.

Since you are just starting and funds are tight, it is best to keep a workforce of between two (2) to five (5) persons only. But if you can do the job alone, do not hire workers yet. Let your family members help out in the meantime.

As you progress, hire one employee at a time. Have a workforce Plan. Forecast the possible number of personnel you need vis-à-vis the increase of workload, the possible income, and its equivalent expenses.

6. Promote your products or services.

If you want to go online, Facebook offers an affordable promotional arrangement, which can be streamlined for your target demographics. On the other hand, you may also use the traditional promotion techniques such as, tarpaulins, flyers, radio, and TV.

Word of mouth, and referrals depend on the extent to which customers spread the word among their peers, like how great your service was, or how competitive your price. It certainly isn't the most effective prospecting strategy, but it can help.

Discipline

It is easy to plan, but difficult to execute.

Most smart people have perfect plans, and perfect dreams, but remained where they are, because they failed to take action.

Have the discipline to work on your plans. Create a daily checklist.

Plan your week ahead. And revisit your plan every day before going to bed.

Every night, before you sleep, check your list if you've accomplished your tasks for the day. In case you miss something, include it on the next day.

Most successful people in life exercise discipline on a daily basis. It brings stability and structure into a person's life. It teaches a person to be responsible and respectful.

Have the discipline to stick to your schedule. Do not put off your plans for leisure, laziness, or simple complacency.

Deliver what you are expected to deliver today. Your future self will thank you for it.

Great leaders constantly display restraint. Not giving into whims is a sign of strength. Making the right decisions can make or break you, and persons with self-restraint tends to make the right decisions.

"Discipline is the bridge between goals and accomplishment."

APPENDIX A

Below is a simplified business plan I used in all the businesses I have created. Information supplied are for illustration purposes only.

If you want to use the complete and extensive format, you may research the internet for samples.

(Name of Business)

I   Rationale / the opportunity

(You state here the situation or things that pushed you to start your own business)

Example

Children nowadays, starting age two (2) are addicted to cell phones and tablets. This has a negative impact on their health.

As such, an orientation seminar for parents to inform them of the imminent danger of gadgets to their children is timely.

Or

As such, an alternative toy for children not hazardous to their health but equally entertaining is a suitable solution.

II   Objectives:

(You state here your vision. Your dream)

Example

A successful and profitable consulting, or services firm that helps parents raise upright and healthy children.

or

A profitable toy manufacturing company that specializes in toys that enhances children's cognitive abilities.

III.   The business

(Describe here the business you want to build. This is the backbone of your business plan. I simplify this part by just using the 5Ps)

Product:
Price:
Promotion:
Place:
People:

(Read Chapter 6 for reference)

III.   Financial plan

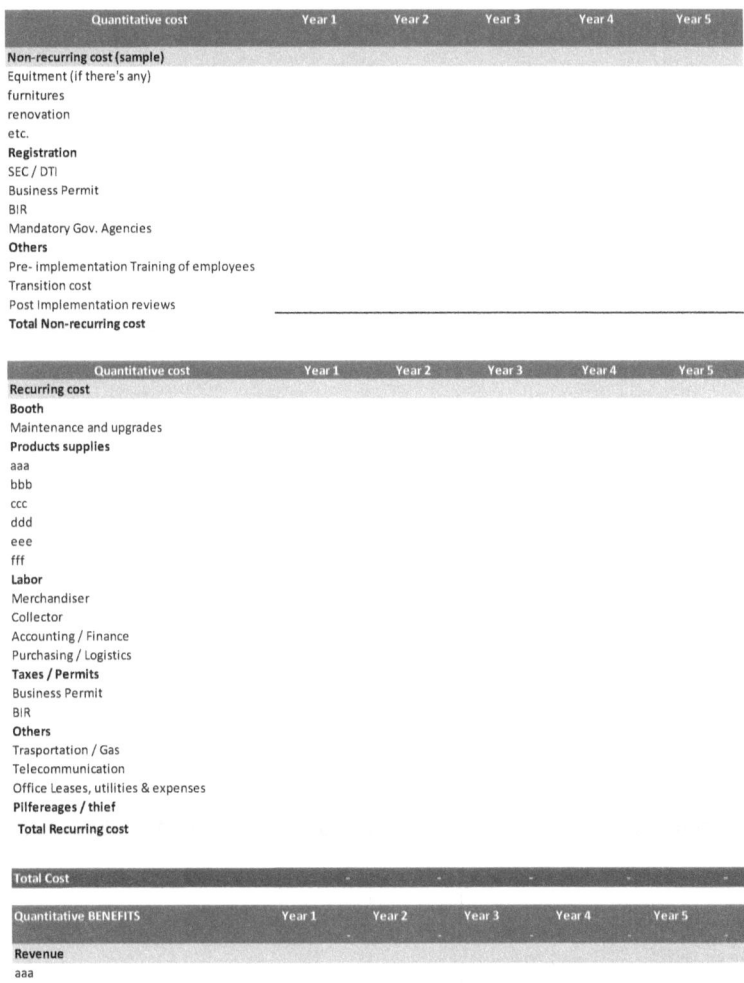

Quantitative cost	Year 1	Year 2	Year 3	Year 4	Year 5
Non-recurring cost (sample)					
Equitment (if there's any)					
furnitures					
renovation					
etc.					
Registration					
SEC / DTI					
Business Permit					
BIR					
Mandatory Gov. Agencies					
Others					
Pre- implementation Training of employees					
Transition cost					
Post Implementation reviews					
Total Non-recurring cost					

Quantitative cost	Year 1	Year 2	Year 3	Year 4	Year 5
Recurring cost					
Booth					
Maintenance and upgrades					
Products supplies					
aaa					
bbb					
ccc					
ddd					
eee					
fff					
Labor					
Merchandiser					
Collector					
Accounting / Finance					
Purchasing / Logistics					
Taxes / Permits					
Business Permit					
BIR					
Others					
Trasportation / Gas					
Telecommunication					
Office Leases, utilities & expenses					
Pilfereages / thief					
Total Recurring cost					

Total Cost	-	-	-	-	-

Quantitative BENEFITS	Year 1	Year 2	Year 3	Year 4	Year 5
Revenue					
aaa					
bbb					
ccc					
ddd					
eee					
fff					
Total Revenues					
Total benefits	-	-	-	-	-

* I use the cost benefit analysis to determine the profitability of my business plan. You may use the intensive financial plan format you are comfortable with.

APPENDIX B

Three main types of businesses in the Philippines:

Sole Proprietorship:

A Sole proprietorship is the most basic type of business organization, you can run in the Philippines. It can be established by just one person, referred to as a sole proprietor. Essentially, your business in a sole proprietorship is an extension of yourself, so the assets and liabilities of your business are also your own assets and liabilities.

Partnership: A partnership requires two or more people who agree to contribute assets, with the intent of dividing profits among all parties involved.

Corporation: A corporation is comprised of at least five (5) individuals who act as a single entity to advance the interest of the corporation as a whole. A Corporation, like partnership has a separate personality from its stockholders and is treated by law as a juridical person.

How to Register a Sole Proprietorship?

The Philippine law treats the owner and the business as the same, the sole proprietor only needs to register his or her name with the Department of Trade and Industry (DTI) and secure local licenses and permits to commence business operations.

1. Register a business name with the DTI
2. Register with the Barangay Office where the business is going to be located
3. Register with the Mayor's Office
4. Register with the Bureau of Internal Revenue (BIR)

How to register a Partnership

A Partnership is a separate legal entity from that of the partners in the partnership. A partnerships consist of 2 or more individuals, and may either be a; general partnership, where partners have unlimited liability for the debts and obligation of the partnership, or a limited partnership, where one or more of the partners have unlimited liability and some partners have liability only up to the amount of their capital contributions.

Requirements

1. Registration with SEC
2. Submission of duly notarized Articles of Partnership
3. Submission of SEC form F-105 (for partnerships with foreign members)
4. Procurement of licenses and clearances from necessary government offices
5. Registration with BIR
6. Acquisition of business permit and mayor's license
7. Registration with mandatory government offices (if employing individuals)
   - Social Security System (SSS)
   - Philippine Health Insurance Corporation (PhilHealth)
   - Home Development Mutual Fund (HDMF or Pag-Ibig Fund)

How to register a Corporation

Registration process for domestic corporations:

1. Registration of proposed company name with the SEC
2. Submission of documentary requirements of the SEC such as:
   - Articles of Incorporation and Bylaws
   - Treasurer's Affidavit
   - Bank Certificate showing the paid-up capital

- Registration Data Sheet
- Clearances from other government agencies (if applicable)
- Registration of Stock and Transfer Books

3. Registration with the Bureau of Internal Revenue (BIR)
4. Procurement of business permits and licenses from the city or municipality where the business will be located
5. Procurement of secondary licenses if the business will engage in regulated industry sectors
6. Registering with mandatory government agencies such as the following:
   - Social Security System (SSS)
   - Philippine Health Insurance Corporation (PhilHealth)
   - Home Development Mutual Fund (HDMF or Pag-Ibig Fund)

Thank you very much.

Good luck on your business endeavors!

God bless!

About the Author

Delyen Madula is a consultant at Madula Rousseau Consulting, a consultancy firm that specializes in providing expert assistance to foreign or local organizations and/or individuals, doing business or planning to do business in the Philippines, in their new or existing Business documentation requirements, from business registration, to other related Corporate services, as well as policies related to the Philippines Data Privacy Act (DPA) and the EU General Data Protection Regulation (GDPR).

She is also an entrepreneur with businesses in IT, Construction, and in retail. She has a Pre-law academic degree of Bachelors of Science in Business Administration, and a Postgraduate academic degree of Bachelors of Law.

She loves to write books about business and related laws, real life inspirational stories, and legal fiction. Her first book "How to start a business with no money" was inspired by her persona in starting up her businesses. She has more books underway, one is a legal fiction, another is a real life inspiring story, and a sequel to her first book.

Madula Rousseau Consulting

Madula Rousseau Business Managements Consulting Services provides expert assistance to foreign or local organizations and/or individuals, doing business or planning to do business in the Philippines, in their new or existing Business documentation requirements, from business registration, to other related Corporate services, as well as policies related to the Philippines Data Privacy Act (DPA) and the EU General Data Protection Regulation (GDPR).

Our consultants are experienced, knowledgeable and exceptional specialists and entrepreneurs who are significantly well versed with Business /Commercial laws, Taxation laws, and other related Rules and Regulations in the Philippines, and Europe.

We offer consultancy for:

• Existing businesses

• Start-up businesses

Our services include:

- Business Registration
- Product / Brand Registration
- Tax Services & Consulting
- Bookkeeping & Payroll
- Labor / Human Resources Consulting
- Regulatory affairs Consulting

- European Business Entry Plan to the Philippines
- Visa and immigration processing services
- Cyber Security Risks and Strategy
- Personal and Commercial Data Protection and Governance.

What can you expect?

Madula Rousseau Consulting has:

- Expertise in European and Filipino laws and regulatory affairs.

- Expertise in data protection (GDPR and DPA)

- Expertise in cyber security

- Interlocutors in the Philippines and Europe

For consultation, email us at
madularousseau@yahoo.com

www.ingramcontent.com/pod-product-compliance
Lightning Source LLC
Chambersburg PA
CBHW020602220526
45463CB00006B/2413